# HONG KONG, BALI & SINGAPORE

## A PICTURE BOOK TO REMEMBER HER BY

Designed by
### DAVID GIBBON

Produced by
### TED SMART

CRESCENT

# INTRODUCTION

In the first half of the nineteenth century Lord Palmerston contemptuously described Hong Kong as a "barren island with hardly a house upon it". Today it is a crowded, prosperous island with hardly enough space for all the people who want to live there. Building is upward rather than outward and steep hillsides are terraced in order to provide additional usable land. There are even a quarter of a million people, the famous "Boat People" who live afloat, many of whom seldom set foot on dry land. But the Crown Colony of Hong Kong is not just the one island; on the mainland to the north, beyond the concrete jungles of the Kowloon peninsula and the mountains of the Nine Dragons, are nearly 800 square kilometres of mountains and valleys known as the New Territories which are held from China on a ninety-nine-year lease granted in 1898. Out to sea is an archipelago of 230 beautiful and mainly uninhabited islands. In the New Territories the way of life has changed remarkably little; men and animals still live in walled villages and every scrap of land, however unpromising, is cultivated. The bright green rice fields and terraced farmlands make a patchwork of brilliant colours on the doorstep of China and from the thirteenth century village of Kam Tin one can look across the bamboo curtain into the great People's Republic. But Hong Kong island is indubitably the focus of life in the area. Its capital, Victoria, is full of streets teeming with people, rickshaws, cars and taxis, with skyscrapers side by side with grand old colonial buildings. Gaily-coloured washing is festooned from balconies like bunting and from every factory there is the hum of feverish activity which accounts for the affluence of this tiny colony in the South China Sea. Hong Kong is a free port whose harbour is always thronged with sampans, junks, cargo lighters and ferryboats, as well as ocean-going liners and tankers which facilitate the trade so vital to her survival. In the harbour the visitor is aware of the crowded typhoon shelters so important in an area which suffers every year from these violent winds which blow across the China Sea at the end of the hot summer. When a typhoon is forecast the larger ships make for deep sea anchorages and the smaller ones make for the shelters; ashore, shops are boarded up and everyone waits for the inevitable destruction. When the typhoon arrives it uproots trees, overturns cars, smashes windows, rips neon signs and tin roofs from buildings and destroys unprotected sampans and junks. However, life must return to normal as soon as possible so that the life-blood of trade can continue.

Like Hong Kong, Singapore is an important centre of trade and commerce. Yet only 150 years ago Singapore, a tiny island at the southern tip of the Malay Peninsula, was a swampy jungle, where the only settlements were a few scattered fishing villages and the population consisted of eighty Malays and half as many Chinese. An Englishman, Stamford Raffles, recognised that Singapore could become the oriental counterpart of Malta as an international trading centre and leased the island from the Sultan of Johore on behalf of the East India Company. He immediately began to build, and from this early beginning the huge city and port we see today has grown. The harbour is constantly crowded with shipping ranging from liners to sailing boats. The larger vessels may unload in the docks or anchor offshore and discharge their cargoes into sampans. The city presents a fascinating blend of Eastern and Western cultures and modern buildings blend with the ornate mosques and temples of the old city. But the predominant lifestyle is that of the Chinese, who make up over three-quarters of the population of Singapore. Recent development to meet the demands of rising population and industrialisation has resulted in the disappearance of more and more old features of the island to make way for apartment blocks, schools, hospitals and factories. At this rate the quaint old fishing villages and plantations of tapioca and coconut palms will eventually cease to exist so that Singapore can keep pace with the twentieth century.

Unlike Singapore and Hong Kong, Bali has been little altered by the modern world. This picturesque volcanic island belongs to the Republic of Indonesia and is separated from Java by the narrow Bali Strait. Much of the island is uninhabited, the vegetation is green and lush and there are fine sandy beaches which are protected by coral reefs. The Balinese people are noted for their fine physique and the women are renowned for their beauty. The religion is Hinduism which was brought by settlers from India in the seventh century but the Balinese beliefs are not entirely involved with the gods but are also concerned with the spirits of their ancestors. Religious ceremonies and festivals, and musical and theatrical performances, are all carried out in the hope that the all-important spirits will not become dissatisfied with life on the island and leave. Festivals are numerous and provide colourful spectacles; Balinese women wearing brightly-coloured batik sarongs form processions bearing offerings of food and flowers piled high on their heads and walk with remarkable skill and grace to the many temples and shrines which are scattered throughout the island. Bali boasts many skilled craftsmen, including experts at creating exquisite objects out of gold and silver, wood and stone. Traditional delicacies are roast sucking pig and duckling baked in banana leaves, served with bowls of steaming rice flavoured with exotic sauces, and accompanied by either a sweet rice wine or by arak, which is distilled from coconut sap. A visit to the market at Denpasar, the island's capital, is an unforgettable experience. In this colourful, aromatic place all manner of things ranging from dried fish to incense, from clay pots to fighting cocks, are sold. Since Bali was "discovered" by the western world in the 1930s tourism has become an important part of the island's life but instead of spoiling the island's indigenous culture, tourism has happily enhanced and strengthened it.

*Left:* Sunset over junks and sampans in Hong Kong Harbour.

4

# HONG KONG

A marvellous panorama *above* showing the modern skyscrapers of Hong Kong and Kowloon and one of the finest harbours in the world.

Many of Hong Kong's buildings date back to the old colonial days. One of them *left,* is the gracious, domed Supreme Court. Other buildings include the Hong Kong Club, the Cricket Club and the new Connaught Centre.

Hong Kong is an island of a million lights and the brilliant night views shown on this page and overleaf are unforgettable.

5

7

In the late, hot summer, the mighty typhoons – those violent, revolving storms – roar across the China Sea and create havoc. The fragile junks and sampans scurry to the typhoon shelters *above and left* and the larger ships make for deeper anchorages, whilst ashore, buildings are boarded up and cars and buses garaged.

Hong Kong is a British Crown Colony and the traffic still drives on the left. Numerous trams, buses, mini-buses and cars cause extensive traffic jams on the overcrowded island.

The dazzling lights of Hong Kong and Kowloon *overleaf* illuminate a myriad of shops, restaurants, offices and apartment blocks.

One of the sights of Hong Kong Island is Victoria Peak, which towers above the tallest buildings. Reached by funicular railway, it affords breathtaking views of a large part of Hong Kong. On the Peak are the famous and exotic Tiger Balm Gardens with their ornate White Pagoda and the fascinating statues depicting scenes from Chinese legends. The gardens reflect the oriental passion for precision in their landscaping.

The atmosphere and excitement of the East is to be found in the bustling street markets of Hong Kong. Here, there is a confusion of neon signs, rickshaws and shoppers as well as the colour and variety of the stalls themselves. Every kind of fruit and vegetable is on sale as well as cooked delicacies, and the plastic toys for which the island is internationally famous, and tempting duty-free goods may also be purchased.

15

These colourful photographs show two of Hong Kong's palatial floating restaurants, one at Sha Tin, Kowloon *above*, and the other *left* at Aberdeen, Hong Kong Island. This is where the Boat People, known as Tanka, live and some of them earn extra money by ferrying tourists to these restaurants – where they, the tourists, eat expensively and overlook the picturesque but hard way of life of the Tanka.

*Overleaf:* Nathan Road, Kowloon, at night. Because of the proximity of Kaitak Airport, the neon lights never flash.

More views of Hong Kong's busy, crowded streets, where double-decker London buses are a familiar sight. A rickshaw coolie *below* awaits a fare. Like the sedan-chair, rickshaws are fast becoming an obsolete form of transport.

The bi-lingual street-signs *right* advertise fabric shops, where some of the world's finest materials, especially silk, are on display. The skilled Chinese tailors of Hong Kong are renowned for supplying suits and dresses, made-to-measure in just a few hours.

21

Hong Kong's harbours are a labyrinth of junks and sampans, cargo ships, yachts and ferry boats. Every day, tons of rice as well as thousands of live pigs and fruit and vegetables are sent from that vast country – the People's Republic of China – to Hong Kong, and all must be unloaded. The photographs on these pages show men, women and children busily going about this work in their sampans.

23

Hong Kong has many lovely beaches such as Shek O *left* – a retreat for thousands of weekend sun-worshippers.

The beach *above* of Stanley Village and *right* two views of Repulse Bay, also on the southern side of Hong Kong Island, overlooked by the gracious old Repulse Bay Hotel.

The New Territories *overleaf* is the area of Hong Kong closest to China. It is a beautiful region of mountains and valleys, jungle and bamboo glades. This is the home of the Hakka farming people, who live in ancient walled villages with their animals. They cultivate every possible scrap of land, much of which is flooded for rice-growing and fish and duck farming.

25

28

The Dragon Boat Festival *right* is the most riotous of the Chinese waterborne festivals. It entails many teams, each paddling long dragon boats in earnestly competed races. Many of the boats capsize during the racing.

The wide bay at Tolo *left* in the New Territories, and *below left* the familiar sight of fishing boats at Castle Peak Bay, in the same region.

The Man Mo Temple *above* in Hollywood Road is dedicated to two gods – King-Emperor Mun Cheong, the civil god – and the Holy King-Emperor Kwan, the martial god.

Some of the treasures *right* of the Temple of Ten Thousand Buddhas at Sha Tin, another of Hong Kong's numerous temples.

29

Sunset over the harbour *left* and *above* the distinctive sails of a junk.

The Wong Tai Sin low-cost resettlement area in Kowloon *below left* and *below* Ocean Terminal, Asia's largest shopping complex.

# BALI

Bali has caught the imagination of the world, and not least through the spectacular dances, in great variety, that are performed there every day. As may easily be seen, the dancers, in their magnificent costumes display an elegance of movement that enhances their already remarkable beauty, and they leave a lasting impression on the visitor.

The many dances tell stories related to Balinese history, and the traditions are strictly observed. The picture at the top of the page shows three young girls performing the Legong Dance – a story of a king and a captured princess of long ago.

Tropical produce grows to perfection on this volcanic island. Rice forms part of the staple diet and has a continuous growing season. The crop being harvested *above*, and in various stages of cultivation *left and both pictures below*.

A magnificent example of the Balinese landscape *overleaf* where terracing ensures that every available piece of land is cultivated.

35

Bali has a beautiful and often dramatic coastline as shown *below* in the view taken at Ulu Watu of the beach and cliffs at one of the island's most southerly points.

While women collect driftwood *left* for the cooking-fires the men return *centre and bottom left* after low tide with collected coral which will be cleaned and modelled, ready to sell as souvenirs to the many tourists who visit the island.

Tourists are also likely to be the recipients of the catch that will be the result of the fishing expeditions *right*. The Balinese themselves rarely eat fish.

The Balinese have a most important
religious relationship with the sea for, as
Hindus, they must always ensure that the
ashes of their loved ones are scattered over
the waters after cremation. This explains
their reluctance to eat fish or even to bathe
in the sea. Once a year, however, they hold
a very colourful festival to offer gifts of
fruit to the spirits of the sea as tokens of
their belief and respect.

Cremations take place in a community ceremony of deep religious significance. The soul, freed of its physical limitations, can attain a higher level of awareness and, it is believed, be re-incarnated as a better being.

The island's most important crop, rice, being harvested *right*.

44

Two of the most important and famous of all Balinese dances are shown on these pages. The Ketchak or Monkey Dance *below right and above* is predominantly for men. The other dance *left and above right* is the equally colourful Barong. The Barong dance features a fierce sea-monster tamed by offerings from the Balinese people and it is used in the dance to frighten away evil, represented by Rangda the witch.

One of Bali's beautiful and imposing temples *overleaf*.

A fearsome but exquisite stone carving outside a temple *below*.

A simple temple ceremony *left* involving offerings to a priest and *centre* a small temple that almost seems to float on the water.

A delightful study *bottom left* of a monkey balancing on a stone carving in the Holy Monkey Forest at Sangeh. Here may be found a beautiful forest of pala trees where hundreds of monkeys live. The broad leaves of the trees allow hardly any light to filter through to the forest floor.

A scene *above right* in a typical market where tourists are as welcome as local people. Cock-fighting *right* is a daily event lasting many hours and large sums of money are wagered on the outcome of each encounter.

Everywhere there are constant reminders of the beauty of the tropical island of Bali and never more so than in the typical gardens *left* and the Golden Room setting *below left.* A village temple *above* has the appearance of being hidden in its jungle setting for centuries. The beautiful Water Palace *below* is situated at Udjung, on the eastern coast.

The fascinating painting *overleaf* depicts many of the facets of life on Bali and features particularly the Barong Dance at its centre.

# SINGAPORE

Singapore – where the old and the new mingle on a thriving but tiny green island at the tip of the Malay Peninsula. The famous Raffles Hotel *top left* was named after the man who founded Singapore in the early 19th century.

The modern waterfront is shown *far left. Above* is an aerial view of the city with the Singapore River in the background, which is, today, one of the busiest waterways in the world. In contrast is the modern Hotel Apollo *left*, built to cope with the enormous influx of tourists and business people who flock to the island.

*Overleaf:* The Esplanade, Singapore.          55

The famous outdoor restaurants *left* in
Bugis Street, where mouth-watering
dishes are cooked in minutes. Singapore
is world-famous for its cuisine which is
of infinite variety. On this page is shown
food being prepared *below* at the Satay
Club and *bottom right* tourists enjoying
a meal in the Dragon Palace Restaurant
in the Cockpit Hotel.

In more informal surroundings diners
relax *centre right* at an outdoor
restaurant and local people *top right*
select items from a fresh-fruit stall.

On these pages are shown scenes of the fantastically cosmopolitan life of Singapore – a city of excitement that seems almost unable to sleep. An Indian cultural dance is shown *far left, top* and *far left, centre* are shown two beautiful local girls. A Malay wedding party is pictured *far left, bottom* in colourful costume and *near left, top* is one of the great tourist attractions – two snake-charmers enticing cobras from their baskets.

A colourful market scene *left* and an equally colourful scene from a Chinese opera *above*. Contrasting shop interiors are depicted *top right and right* and the excitement and colour of a procession during the Chinese New Year is shown *centre right*.

62

A must for all visitors is surely Haw Par Villa *left*. Here may be seen the temple in its luxuriant surroundings whilst *below left* children explore the almost 'fairy grotto' exhibits.

Contrasting styles of two local lantern-makers are shown *above and right*. *Centre right* is a scene taken at the famous Kusu Festival. The blur and excitement of night-time traffic in Singapore is shown *top right* and the tranquil and eternal setting sun *overleaf*.

63

First published in Great Britain 1978 by Colour Library International Ltd.
© Illustrations: Colour Library International Ltd. Colour separations by La Cromolito, Milan, Italy.
Display and text filmsetting by Focus Photoset, London, England.
Printed and bound by L.E.G.O. Vicenza, Italy.
Published by Crescent Books, a division of Crown Publishers Inc.
Library of Congress Catalogue Card No. 78-60452
**CRESCENT 1978**